I0410863

Contents

Sales of Fossil Fuels Produced from Federal and Indian Lands, FY 2003 through FY 2013 1

    Summary...1

    Sales from production on federal and Indian lands 4

    Trends in federal and Indian lands production from FY 2003 through FY 2013......................5

    State/offshore trends 7

    Data sources 10

Appendix 23

    State/area maps 23

Tables

Table 1. Fossil fuel sales of production from federal lands, FY 2003-13 2

Table 2. Fossil fuel sales of production from Indian lands, FY 2003-13 3

Table 3. Sales of crude oil and lease condensate production from federal and Indian lands, FY 2003-13 16

Table 4. Sales of natural gas production from federal and Indian lands, FY 2003-13 16

Table 5. Sales of natural gas plant liquids production from federal and Indian lands, FY 2003-13 17

Table 6. Sales of fossil fuel production from federal and Indian lands by state/area, FY 2003-13 18

Table 7. Sales of crude oil and lease condensate production from federal and Indian lands by state/area, FY 2003-13 19

Table 8. Sales of natural gas production from federal and Indian lands by state/area, FY 2003-13 20

Table 9. Sales of natural gas plant liquids production from federal and Indian lands by state/area, FY 2003-13 21

Table 10. Sales of coal production from federal and Indian lands by state, FY 2003-13 22

Figures

Figure 1. Fossil fuel production on federal lands, FY 2003-13 6

Figure 2. Fossil fuel production on Indian lands, FY 2003-13 7

Figure 3. Onshore federal and Indian lands 8

Figure 4. Fossil fuel production on federal and Indian lands, FY 2003-13 10

Figure 5. Crude oil production on federal and Indian lands, FY 2003-13 12

Figure 6. Natural gas production on federal and Indian lands, FY 2003-13 13

Figure 7. Natural gas liquids production on federal and Indian lands, FY 2003-13 14

Figure 8. Coal production on federal and Indian lands, FY 2003-13 15

Figure A1. Fossil fuel production on federal and Indian lands, FY 2013 23

Figure A2. Changes in fossil fuels production (trillion Btu) on federal and Indian lands, FY 2003-13 24

Figure A3. Crude oil production on federal and Indian lands, FY 2013 25

Figure A4. Changes in crude oil production on federal and Indian lands, FY 2003-13 26

Figure A5. Natural gas production on federal and Indian lands, FY 2013 27

Figure A6. Changes in natural gas production on federal and Indian lands, FY 2003-13 28

Figure A7. Natural gas liquids production on federal and Indian lands, FY 2013 29

Figure A8. Changes in natural gas liquids production on federal and Indian lands, FY 2003-13 30

Figure A9. Coal production on federal and Indian lands, FY 2013 31

Figure A10. Changes in coal production on federal and Indian lands, FY 2003-13 32

Sales of Fossil Fuels Produced from Federal and Indian Lands, FY 2003 through FY 2013

Summary

The U.S. Energy Information Administration (EIA) estimates that total sales of fossil fuels from production[1] on federal and Indian lands decreased by 7% during fiscal year[2] (FY) 2013. The decrease in production on federal lands alone was also 7% (Table 1). Sales from production on Indian lands, which account for less than 7% of total federal and Indian lands production, increased by 9% (Table 2).

Crude oil production on federal lands increased slightly in FY 2013, but that increase was more than offset by decreases in coal, natural gas, and natural gas plant liquids (NGPL) production. Other notable developments in FY 2013 included the following:

- The continued steady decline of offshore natural gas production in the federal Gulf of Mexico (Table 4), a mature area with declining natural gas production from existing fields
- A 9% drop in federal onshore natural gas production, with most of that decrease in Wyoming
- A 9% drop in coal production

Breakdowns by state and area of the fuel production volumes on federal and Indian lands show that:

- Wyoming and the federal Gulf of Mexico together produced 73% of the federal and Indian lands fossil fuels total in FY 2013 (Table 6).[3]
- The federal Gulf of Mexico produced 69% of the federal and Indian lands crude oil total in FY 2013 (Table 7).
- Wyoming, the federal Gulf of Mexico, New Mexico, and Colorado together represented 86% of total production of natural gas on federal and Indian lands in FY 2013 (Table 8).
- Wyoming produced 80% of the federal and Indian lands coal total in FY 2013 (Table 10).

EIA's estimates are based on data provided by the Department of the Interior's (DOI) Office of Natural Resources Revenue (ONRR) and include sales of production from federal onshore and offshore lands, and from Indian lands.[4] EIA summarizes total sales of fossil fuels produced on federal and Indian lands in common energy units (British thermal units, or Btu) to allow for aggregation across fuels, including crude oil and lease condensate, natural gas, natural gas plant liquids, and coal (Tables 1 and 2). The data presented in this paper update data previously reported by EIA[5] for FY 2003 through FY 2012.

The sales reported by ONRR are a reasonable proxy for marketed production for a fiscal year. Sales are assigned to the fiscal year in which the sales were made rather than when royalties were collected. They also include production leaving the lease that is exempt from royalty payments under various royalty relief programs.

---

[1] Throughout this report, the term *production* means sales from production.

[2] The U.S. government's fiscal year runs from October 1 through September 30.

[3] For state-level summaries, ONRR combines Indian and federal lands data to avoid revealing proprietary data.

[4] Includes offshore and onshore areas the federal government owns or administers, including American Indian lands.

[5] Sales of Fossil Fuels Produced from Federal and Indian Lands, FY 2003 through FY 2012, EIA, May 2013, found at
http://www.eia.gov/analysis/requests/federallands/pdf/eia-federallandsales.pdf

Table 1. Fossil fuel sales of production from federal lands, FY 2003-13

Fiscal Year	Crude Oil and Lease Condensate			Natural Gas Plant Liquids [2]			Natural Gas			Coal			Fossil Fuels	
	Million Barrels [1]	Trillion Btu	Percent of U.S. Total	Million Barrels [1]	Trillion Btu	Percent of U.S. Total	Billion Cubic Feet [1]	Trillion Btu	Percent of U.S. Total	Million Short Tons [1]	Trillion Btu	Percent of U.S. Total	Trillion Btu	Percent of U.S. Total
2003	679	3,939	33.0%	93	346	14.7%	6,799	6,982	35.7%	436	8,960	40.6%	20,228	36.1%
2004	670	3,884	33.3%	103	385	15.7%	6,376	6,545	34.0%	451	9,226	41.0%	20,041	35.8%
2005	638	3,698	32.8%	96	358	14.7%	6,057	6,224	33.1%	447	9,110	39.6%	19,390	34.8%
2006	571	3,314	31.3%	85	316	13.8%	5,372	5,522	29.6%	429	8,715	37.2%	17,867	32.4%
2007	618	3,583	33.3%	103	382	16.0%	5,558	5,709	29.2%	443	9,017	38.6%	18,690	33.2%
2008	565	3,276	30.7%	103	382	15.4%	5,535	5,684	27.6%	483	9,771	41.6%	19,112	33.3%
2009	647	3,752	33.9%	92	341	13.8%	5,381	5,518	26.1%	462	9,260	41.5%	18,871	33.0%
2010	722	4,190	36.4%	125	459	16.8%	5,087	5,207	24.4%	456	9,177	42.7%	19,032	33.2%
2011	631	3,658	31.1%	122	450	15.5%	4,597	4,699	20.5%	447	9,016	41.1%	17,823	29.9%
2012	601	3,483	26.4%	119	439	13.7%	4,283	4,383	17.9%	442	8,924	42.1%	17,230	27.7%
2013	606	3,517	22.9%	103	378	11.2%	3,843	3,935	15.9%	401	8,112	40.4%	15,942	25.0%

[1] Includes sales volumes for production from federal lands including all classes of land owned by the federal government, including acquired military, Outer Continental Shelf, and public lands.

[2] Includes only those quantities for which the royalties were paid on the basis of the value of the natural gas plant liquids produced. Additional quantities of natural gas plant liquids were produced; however, the royalties paid were based on the value of natural gas processed. These latter quantities are included with natural gas.

Notes: Total fossil fuels equals the sum of crude oil and lease condensate, natural gas plant liquids, natural gas, and coal. In addition, the sales volumes are reported for the fiscal year in which the sales occurred as opposed to the date of the royalty payment. Volumes include fossil fuels for which royalties were paid, as well as those amounts exempt from royalty payments, such as additions to the Strategic Petroleum Reserve.

Sources: **Physical Data:** U.S. Department of the Interior, Office of Natural Resources Revenue, "ONNR Statistical Information Site" (http://statistics.onrr.gov).

Btu Data: U.S. Energy Information Administration. Btu are calculated using average, calendar-year heat rates for production of each fossil fuel, as reported in the *Monthly Energy Review* (February 2014). The total Btu-content per fossil fuel is calculated by multiplying the physical data by the approximate heat content. The fossil fuel total is the sum of the total heat content for crude oil and lease condensate, natural gas plant liquids, natural gas, and coal.

Percent of Total: Percentages are calculated by dividing sales of production from federal by total U.S. production, then multiplying by 100. Fiscal year values for total U.S. production are the sum of October-September values from the *Monthly Energy Review* (February 2014) and reflect EIA's current data updates.

Table 2. Fossil fuel sales of production from Indian lands, FY 2003-13

Fiscal Year	Crude Oil and Lease Condensate			Natural Gas Plant Liquids[2]			Natural Gas			Coal			Fossil Fuels	
	Million Barrels[1]	Trillion Btu	Percent of U.S. Total	Million Barrels[1]	Trillion Btu	Percent of U.S. Total	Billion Cubic Feet[1]	Trillion Btu	Percent of U.S. Total	Million Short Tons[1]	Trillion Btu	Percent of U.S. Total	Trillion Btu	Percent of U.S. Total
2003	10	59	0.5%	2	6	0.3%	283	291	1.5%	30	616	2.8%	972	1.7%
2004	10	58	0.5%	2	7	0.3%	312	320	1.7%	33	667	3.0%	1,052	1.9%
2005	10	59	0.5%	2	7	0.3%	326	335	1.8%	34	698	3.0%	1,100	2.0%
2006	10	56	0.5%	2	8	0.3%	308	317	1.7%	29	593	2.5%	974	1.8%
2007	10	56	0.5%	3	10	0.4%	284	292	1.5%	27	558	2.4%	916	1.6%
2008	10	57	0.5%	3	11	0.4%	272	279	1.4%	26	527	2.2%	874	1.5%
2009	10	61	0.5%	3	10	0.4%	266	273	1.3%	26	521	2.3%	864	1.5%
2010	13	77	0.7%	3	11	0.4%	251	257	1.2%	22	435	2.0%	780	1.4%
2011	20	115	1.0%	3	12	0.4%	254	260	1.1%	22	444	2.0%	831	1.4%
2012	31	181	1.4%	4	14	0.4%	252	258	1.1%	19	383	1.8%	836	1.3%
2013	46	267	1.7%	4	14	0.4%	239	244	1.0%	19	387	1.9%	912	1.4%

[1]Includes sales volumes for production from Indian lands.

[2]Includes only those quantities for which the royalties were paid on the basis of the value of the natural gas plant liquids were produced; however, the royalties paid were based on the value of natural gas processed. These latter quantities are included with natural gas.

Notes: Total fossil fuels equals the sum of crude oil and lease condensate, natural gas plant liquids, natural gas, and coal. In addition, the sales volumes are reported for the fiscal year in which the sales occurred as opposed to the date of the royalty payment. Volumes include fossil fuels for which royalties were paid, as well as those amounts exempt from royalty payments, such as additions to the Strategic Petroleum Reserve.

Sources: **Physical Data:** U.S. Department of the Interior, Office of Natural Resources Revenue, "ONNR Statistical Information Site" (http://statistics.onrr.gov).

Btu Data: U.S. Energy Information Administration. Btu are calculated using average, calendar-year heat rates for production of each fossil fuel, as reported in the *Monthly Energy Review* (February 2014). The total Btu-content per fossil fuel is calculated by multiplying the physical data by the approximate heat content. The fossil fuel total is the sum of the total heat content for crude oil and lease condensate, natural gas plant liquids, natural gas, and coal.

Percent of Total: Percentages are calculated by dividing sales of production from Indian lands by total U.S. production, then multiplying by 100. Fiscal year values for total U.S. production are the sum of October-September values from the *Monthly Energy Review* (February 2014) and reflect EIA's current data updates.

U.S. Energy Information Administration | Sales of Fossil Fuels Produced on Federal and Indian Lands, FY 2003 through FY 2013

3

Sales from production on federal and Indian lands

Coal represented 51% of fossil fuel sales from production on federal lands in FY 2013, measured in common Btu units, followed by natural gas (25%), crude oil (22%), and NGPL (2%). Total fossil fuels sales from production on federal lands decreased 7% from 17,230 trillion Btu in FY 2012 to 15,942 trillion Btu in FY 2013 (Table 1):

- Sales of crude oil[6] from federal lands increased 1% to 606 million barrels in FY 2013. A 1% decrease in federal offshore volumes was more than offset by a 7% increase in the much smaller federal onshore volumes (Table 3). Despite this increase, crude oil production from federal lands as a share of total U.S. crude oil production dropped from 26% in FY 2012 to 23% in FY 2013 (Table 1). This drop in the federal lands share of total production was the result of the 15% increase in total U.S. crude oil production, with the continued growth in production of tight oil outpacing the modest increase in sales from federal lands.[7]

- Sales of natural gas from federal lands decreased 10% in FY 2013 to 3,843 billion cubic feet, with both offshore (13%) and onshore volumes (9%) declining (Table 4). Natural gas production on federal lands dropped to 16% of the U.S. total in FY 2013 from 18% in FY 2012 (Table 1).

- Sales of NGPL produced on federal lands decreased 13% to 103 million barrels in FY 2013, the third consecutive decrease since the peak year (FY 2010) over the period FY 2003 to FY 2013 (Table 5). Nevertheless, FY 2013 NGPL production was at or above levels reported from FY 2003 through FY 2009. Compared with FY 2012, federal onshore volumes dropped 21% in FY 2013, while federal offshore volumes were virtually unchanged.

- Coal sales from production on federal lands decreased by 9% to 401 million short tons in FY 2013, a 17% decrease from its peak in FY 2008 (Table 1), driven primarily by a decline in Wyoming production (Table 10). Coal produced on federal lands accounted for 40% of the U.S. total in FY 2013, down from 42% in FY 2012.

Coal represented 42% of fossil fuel sales from production on Indian lands in FY 2013, measured in common Btu units, followed by crude oil (29%), natural gas (22%), and NGPL (2%). Total fossil fuels sales from production on Indian lands increased 9% from 836 trillion Btu in FY 2012 to 912 trillion Btu in FY 2013 (Table 2), as an increase in crude oil volumes outpaced a decrease in natural gas volumes:

- Sales of crude oil produced on Indian lands increased a fourth consecutive year, by 48% to 46 million barrels in FY 2013 (Table 3), the highest level between FY 2003 and FY 2013.

- Sales of natural gas from Indian lands decreased by 5% to 239 billion cubic feet in FY 2013 (Table 4).

- Sales of NGPL and coal produced on Indian lands were virtually unchanged at 4 million barrels and 19 million short tons, respectively, in FY 2013 (Tables 5 and 6).

---

[6] Throughout this report, the term *crude oil* includes lease condensate.

[7] http://www.eia.gov/dnav/pet/pet_crd_crpdn_adc_mbblpd_a.htm.

Trends in federal and Indian lands production from FY 2003 through FY 2013

Overall fossil fuel production from federal lands generally declined between FY 2003 and FY 2013, down 21% in FY 2013 compared with FY 2003 (Table 1). This trend is primarily the result of a steady decline in federal offshore natural gas production between FY 2003 and FY 2013 and the 9% drop in coal production from federal lands in FY 2013 from FY 2012.

- Crude oil production from federal lands decreased 11% between FY 2003 and FY 2013 (Figure 1, Table 3). Lower production in the federal Gulf of Mexico over that period led to a decrease in federal offshore production of 18%, which outweighed the 33% increase in the much smaller federal onshore volumes over the same period.

- Natural gas production from federal lands has declined steadily, down 43% by FY 2013 (Figure 1, Table 4). The once-larger federal offshore volumes have declined every year through FY 2013, down 74% from FY 2003. That decrease has been only partially offset by the now-larger onshore volumes, which have increased 17% over the period. This declining natural gas production from federal lands coupled with increasing total U.S. natural gas production[8] steadily reduced the federal lands share of total U.S. natural gas production (Table 1).

- NGPL production from federal lands increased 11% between FY 2003 and FY 2013 (Figure 1, Table 5). Following the natural gas trend, the once-larger federal offshore NGPL volumes have declined 14%, while the now-larger onshore NGPL volumes have increased 40% over the period.

- With the notable exceptions of FY 2008 and FY 2013, years of high and low production respectively, coal production from federal lands has generally not deviated much from its average annual level of 445 million short tons (Table 1). Measured from peak to trough, federal land coal volumes declined 17% over FY 2008 to FY 2013. Coal production on private land declined 12% over the same period.[9]

---

[8] http://www.eia.gov/dnav/ng/ng_prod_sum_dcu_NUS_a.htm.
[9] Implied by Table 1. Also see http://www.eia.gov/coal/data.cfm.

Figure 1. Fossil fuel production on federal lands, FY 2003-13

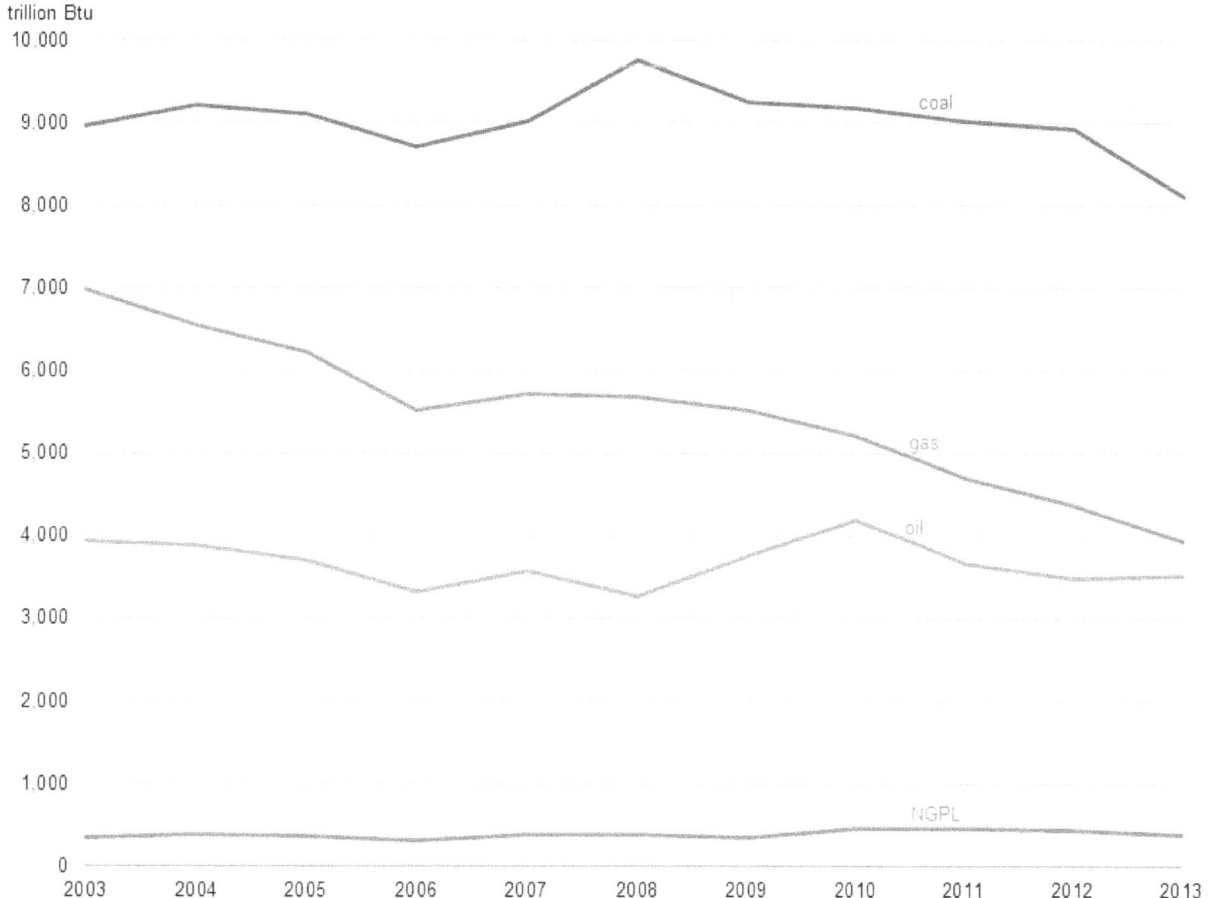

Source: U.S. Energy Information Administration based on U.S. Department of the Interior, Office of Natural Resources Revenue. "ONNR Statistical Information Site" (http://statistics.onrr.gov).

Total fossil fuel production from Indian lands increased each year since FY 2010, although it decreased 6% between FY 2003 and FY 2013. Rapid increases in oil production partially offset large decreases in coal production and smaller decreases in natural gas production between FY 2003 and FY 2013 (Table 2).

- Crude oil production from Indian lands increased 360% from 10 million barrels in FY 2003 to 46 million barrels in FY 2013. Almost all of this increase took place since FY 2010 (Figure 2, Table 3), and mostly in North Dakota (primarily the Fort Berthold Indian Reservation in the western part of the state), with the increase in horizontal drilling and fracking and generally higher oil prices.[10]
- Natural gas production and coal production from Indian lands declined between FY 2003 and FY 2013 by 16% and 37%, respectively. Except for a small deviation in FY 2011, natural gas and coal production have steadily declined since FY 2005 (Table 2).

---

[10] http://www.eia.gov/dnav/pet/hist/LeafHandler.ashx?n=pet&s=rwtc&f=a.

- NGPL production from Indian lands doubled between FY 2003 and FY 2013, although from a low base level (Table 5).

Figure 2. Fossil fuel production on Indian lands, FY 2003-13

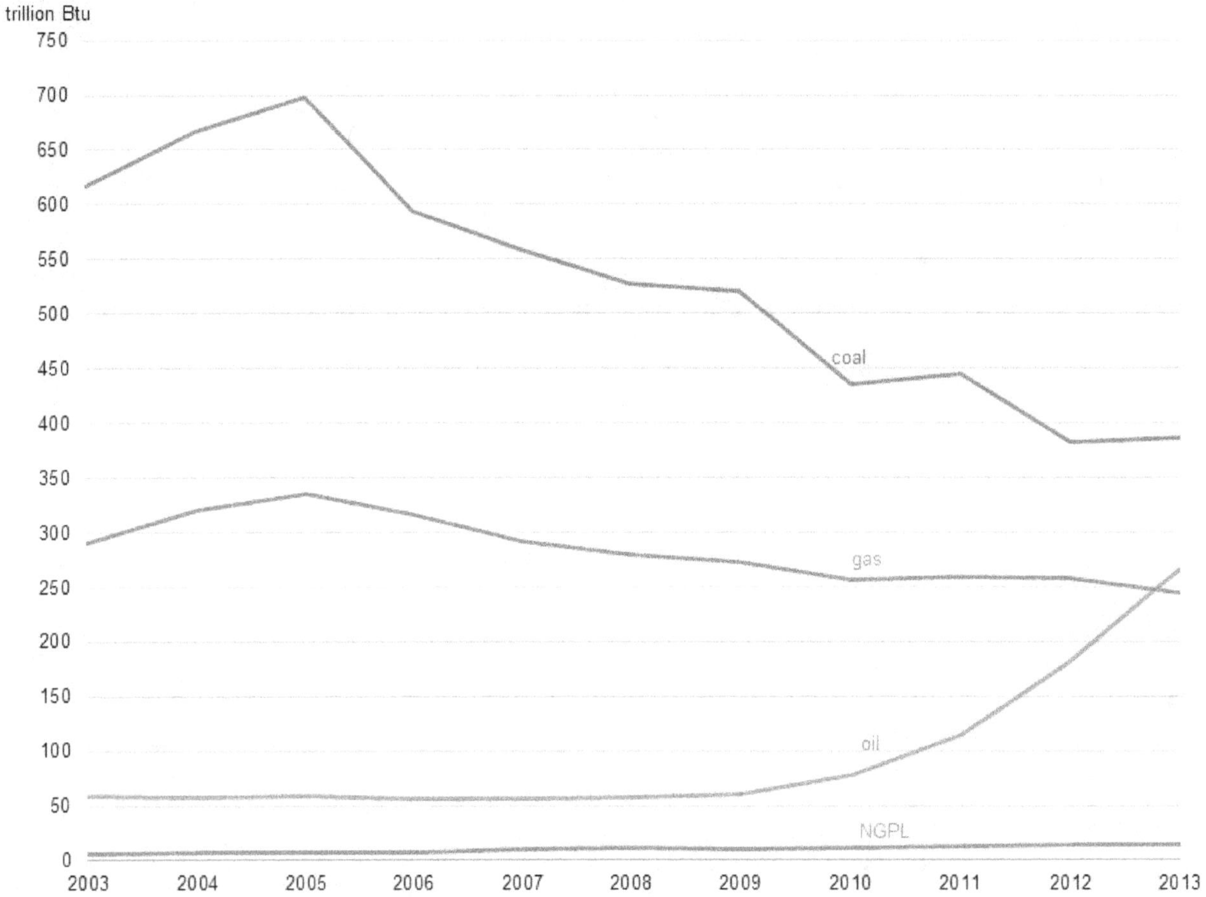

Source: U.S. Energy Information Administration based on U.S. Department of the Interior, Office of Natural Resources Revenue. "ONNR Statistical Information Site" (http://statistics.onrr.gov).

State/offshore trends

The federal government owns nearly 650 million acres of land—almost 30% of the land area of the United States (Figure 3).

Figure 3. Onshore federal and Indian lands

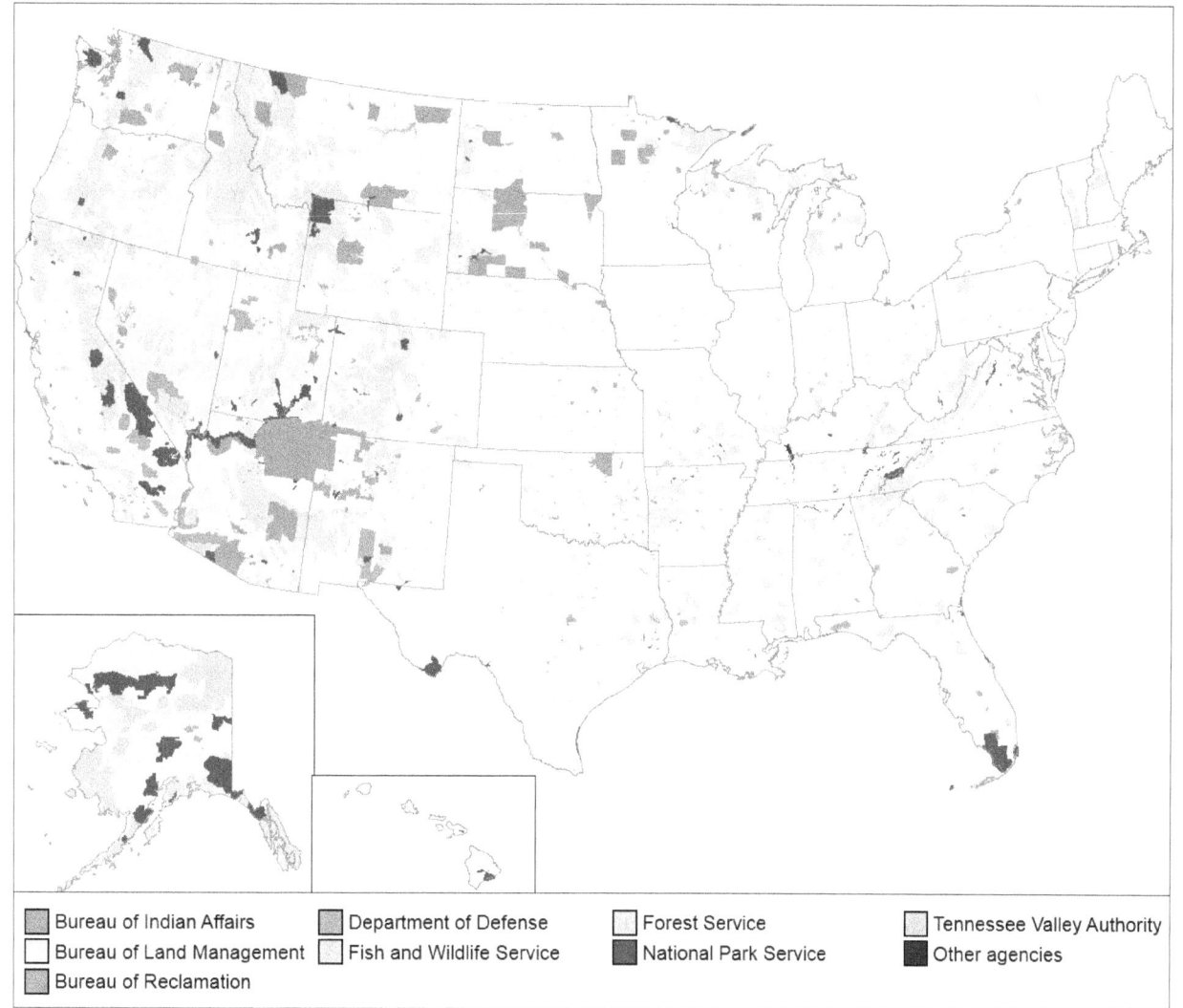

Bureau of Indian Affairs	Department of Defense	Forest Service	Tennessee Valley Authority
Bureau of Land Management	Fish and Wildlife Service	National Park Service	Other agencies
Bureau of Reclamation			

Source: Produced by U.S. Energy Information Administration from Federal Lands and Bureau of Indian Affairs map layers at

http://nationalatlas.gov/maplayers.html?openChapters=chpbound#chpbound

Four agencies—the National Park Service, Fish and Wildlife Service, and Bureau of Land Management (BLM), in the Department of the Interior, and the U.S. Forest Service in the Department of Agriculture—administer about 95% of those federally owned lands.[11],[12]

Most production of fossil fuels from federal and Indian lands falls under purview of the BLM. The BLM manages 248 million acres and is responsible for 700 million acres of subsurface mineral resources.[13]

---

[11] Federal Land Ownership: Current Acquisition and Disposal Authorities, Congressional Research Service, December 13, 2012, found at https://www.fas.org/sgp/crs/misc/RL34273.pdf.

[12] Maps of the various kinds of federal lands can be seen at http://nationalatlas.gov/printable/fedlands.html.

[13] Federal Land Ownership: Overview and Data, Congressional Research Service, February 8, 2012, found at https://www.fas.org/sgp/crs/misc/R42346.pdf.

Federal land ownership is heavily concentrated in 12 western states:

- 62% of Alaska is federally owned.
- 47% of the 11 western states[14] in the Lower 48 is federally owned. In calendar year 2012, those 11 western states represented approximately 20% of total U.S. reserves of crude oil and lease condensate and 24% of total U.S. reserves of wet natural gas.[15] Wyoming, Montana, Colorado, Utah, and New Mexico are the leading states in production of fossil fuels from federal and Indian lands.
- Only 4% of lands in the other states is federally owned.

Indian lands are primarily in the western United States, with concentrations in Arizona; the four corners region of Arizona, New Mexico, Colorado, and Utah; North and South Dakota; and a few other states (Figure 3).

Figures 4 through 8 provide summary information for production from federal and Indian lands for leading states and offshore areas. Complete state-level data on production from federal and Indian lands are provided in Tables 6 through 10.[16] The relative and absolute contribution of each state and offshore region in federal and Indian lands production varies significantly across fuels. Some notable observations include:

- Wyoming and the federal Gulf of Mexico together produced 73% of the federal and Indian lands fossil fuels total in FY 2013 (Table 6, Figure 4). New Mexico, Colorado, and Utah were the next largest production states.
- The federal Gulf of Mexico produced 69% of the federal and Indian lands crude oil total in FY 2013 (Figure 5, Table 7). New Mexico, North Dakota, and Wyoming were the next largest crude oil producers on federal and Indian lands. Crude oil production on federal and Indian lands represents the majority of total (public and private) crude oil production in each of these states: New Mexico, Wyoming, and Utah. [17]
- Rapidly increasing crude oil production from the Bakken formation lifted federal and Indian lands production volumes in North Dakota past corresponding volumes in Wyoming in FY 2013. Federal and Indian lands crude oil production in both North Dakota and New Mexico has been increasing rapidly in recent years.
- Wyoming, the federal Gulf of Mexico, New Mexico, and Colorado together represented 86% of total production of natural gas on federal and Indian lands in FY 2013 (Figure 6, Table 8). The federal Gulf of Mexico's rapidly declining natural gas production fell behind Wyoming by FY 2012. New Mexico's federal and Indian production has declined steadily and gradually over FY 2003 to FY 2013.

---

[14] Montana, Wyoming, Colorado, New Mexico, Idaho, Utah, Arizona, Washington, Oregon, Nevada, California.

[15] U.S. Crude Oil and Natural Gas Proved Reserves, 2012, Tables 6 and 10, EIA, April 2014, found at http://www.eia.gov/naturalgas/crudeoilreserves/.

[16] The Appendix presents information drawn from these tables in the form of maps of the latest state-level production levels and changes.

[17] Calculations based on data at http://www.eia.gov/dnav/pet/pet_crd_crpdn_adc_mbbl_m.htm and "ONNR Statistical Information Site" (http://statistics.onrr.gov)

- • Production of coal on federal and Indian lands is dominated by Wyoming, which accounted for 80% of the total in FY 2013 (Figure 8, Table 10). Montana, Colorado, Utah, and New Mexico were the next biggest coal producers on federal and Indian lands. Production in Wyoming and Montana has been declining since FY 2009, reflecting generally declining demand for coal over the period.

Figure 4. Fossil fuel production on federal and Indian lands, FY 2003-13

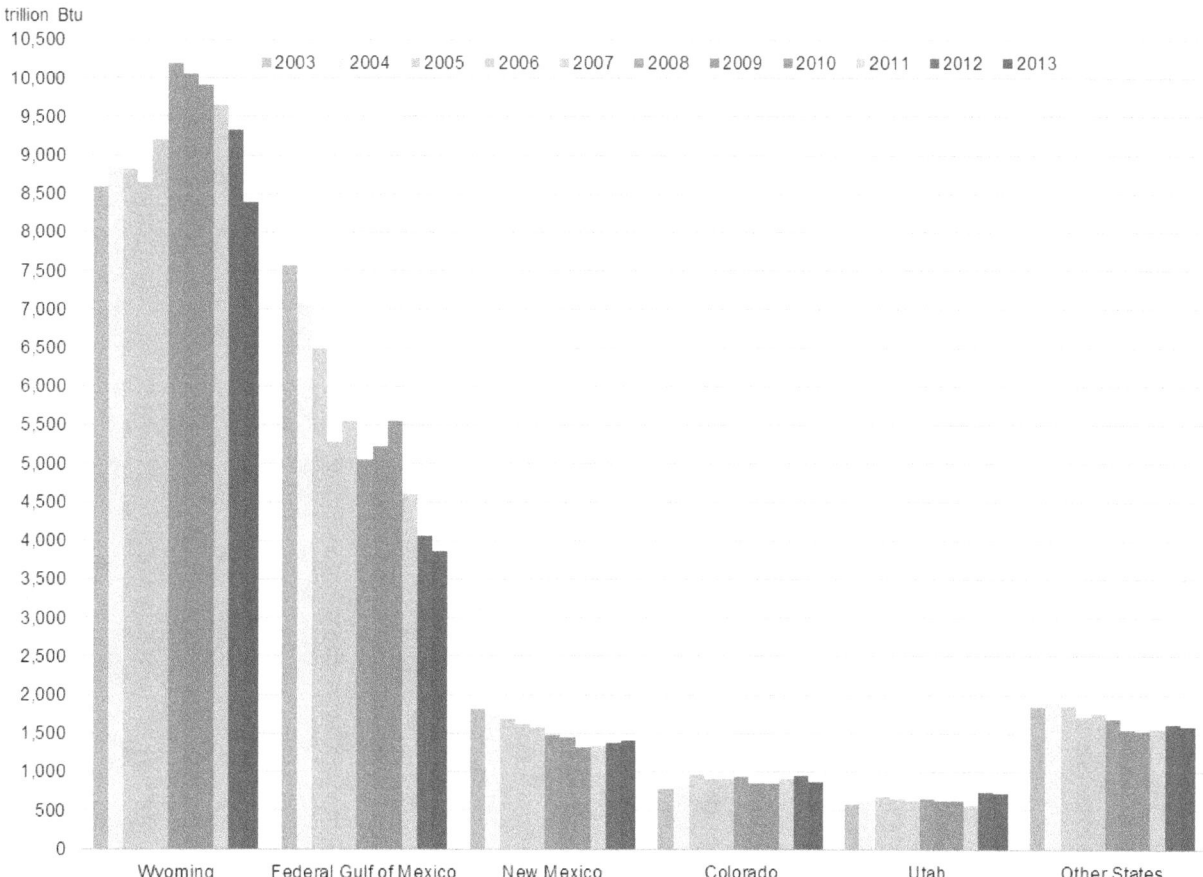

Source: U.S. Energy Information Administration based on U.S. Department of the Interior, Office of Natural Resources Revenue. "ONNR Statistical Information Site" (http://statistics.onrr.gov).

Data sources

Department of Interior program offices continually collect sales and royalty payment data on fossil fuel sales of production from federal and Indian lands. Near the end of the first quarter of each new calendar year, ONRR issues the sales data it collected for the previous sales year. Sales are assigned to the fiscal year in which they occur, not necessarily the same year royalties were collected. Audits conducted by ONNR result in revisions to data previously reported.

This report is based on information reported to and processed by ONRR as of February 5, 2014, and released March 13, 2014. ONRR updates the data values it reports for prior years. The recently-updated data provided by ONRR for FY 2003 through FY 2012 generally fall within 2% of the volumes EIA reported previously, although updates for some NGPL volumes slightly exceeded that threshold (FY 2010 and FY 2011 volumes were revised up about 3% and FY 2012 volumes up about 4%).

Additional data, background information, and discussions of methodology and key drivers contributing to trends in sales from production on federal lands during the FY 2003 through FY 2011 period are available in the earlier EIA report and on the ONRR website.

The following table shows the fuels (commodities) listed on the ONRR website, and the associated products, which were included in this report:

Fuel (commodity)	Product
Coal	Coal
	Coal-Bituminous-Raw
Gas	Coal Bed Methane
	Flash Gas
	Fuel Gas
	Gas Lost - Flared or Vented
	Processed (Residue) Gas
	Unprocessed (Wet) Gas
NGPL	Gas Plant Products
Oil	Condensate
	Drip or Scrubber Condensate
	Fuel Oil
	Inlet Scrubber
	Oil
	Oil Lost
	Other Liquid Hydrocarbons

Figure 5. Crude oil production on federal and Indian lands, FY 2003-13

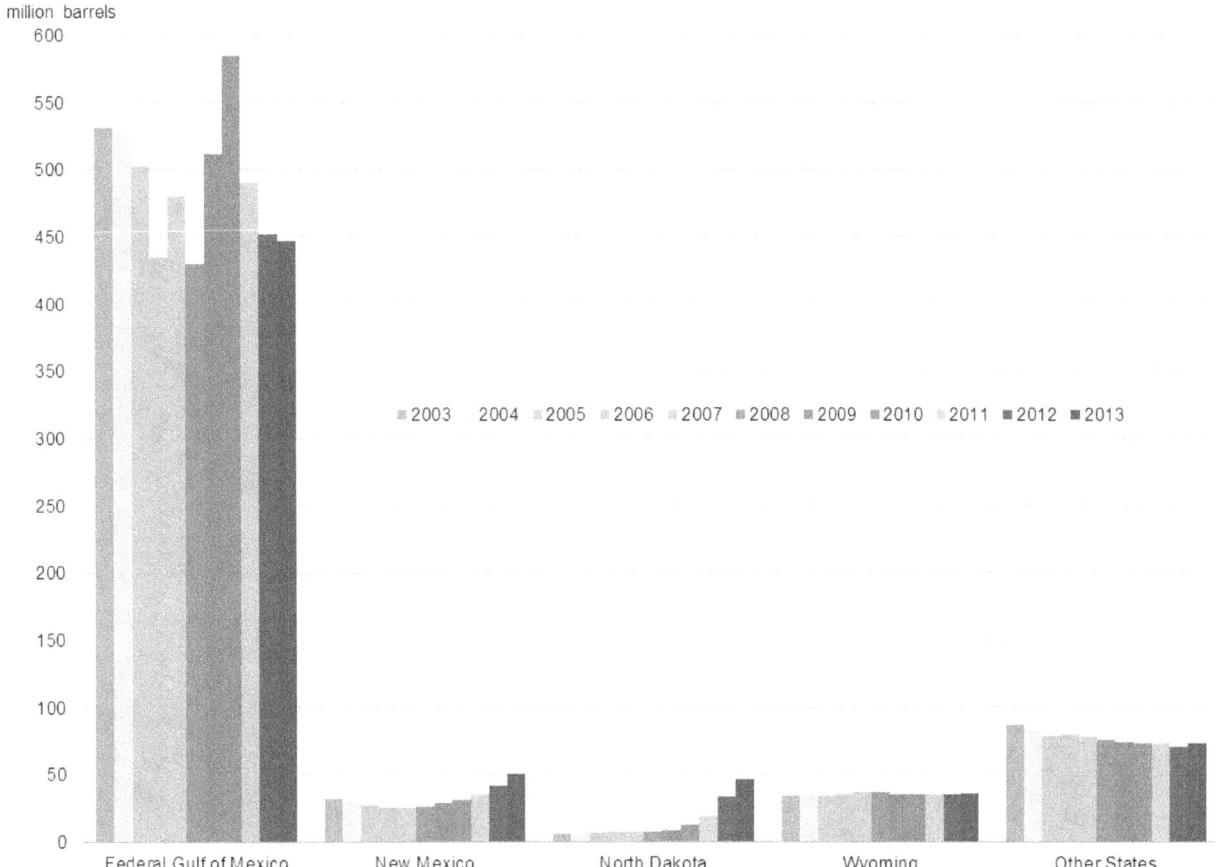

Source: U.S. Energy Information Administration based on U.S. Department of the Interior, Office of Natural Resources Revenue. "ONNR Statistical Information Site" (http://statistics.onrr.gov).

Figure 6. Natural gas production on federal and Indian lands, FY 2003-13

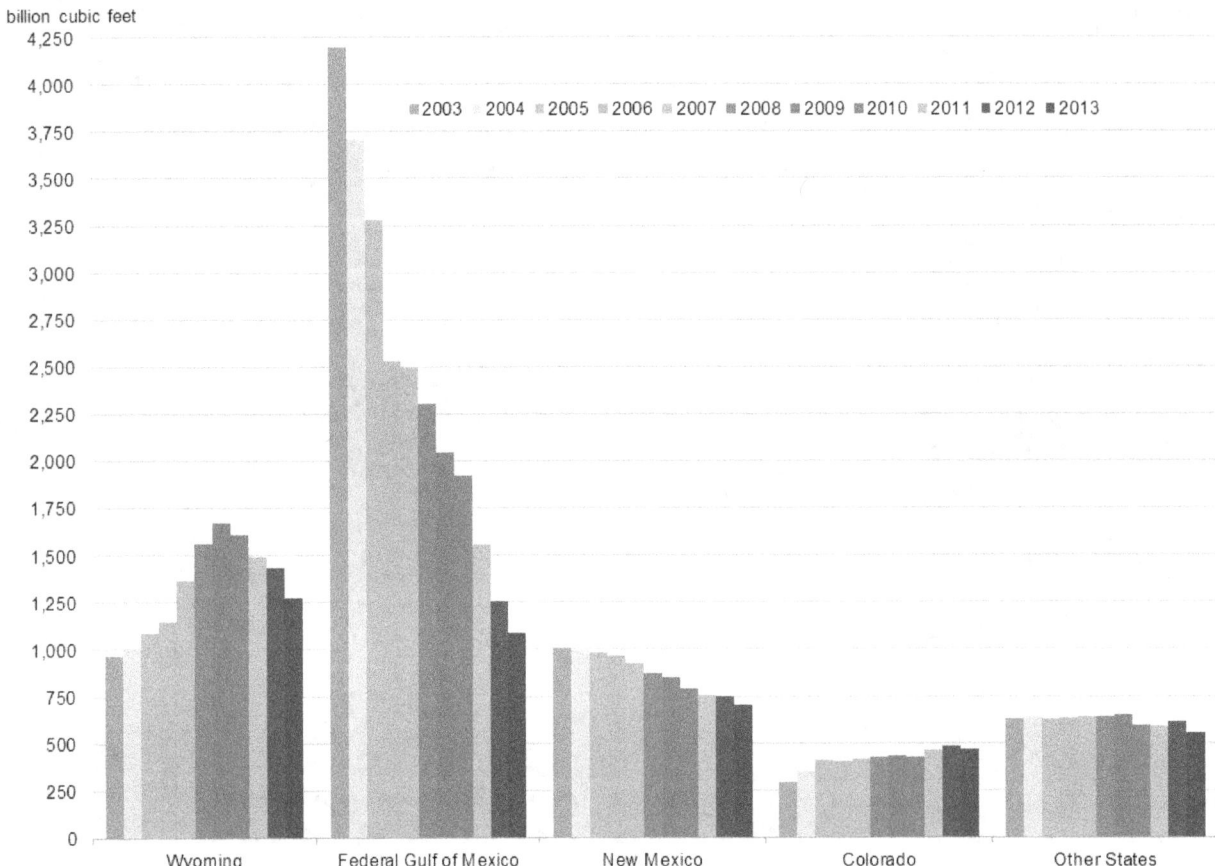

billion cubic feet

Source: U.S. Energy Information Administration based on U.S. Department of the Interior, Office of Natural Resources Revenue. "ONNR Statistical Information Site" (http://statistics.onrr.gov).

Figure 7. Natural gas liquids production on federal and Indian lands, FY 2003-13

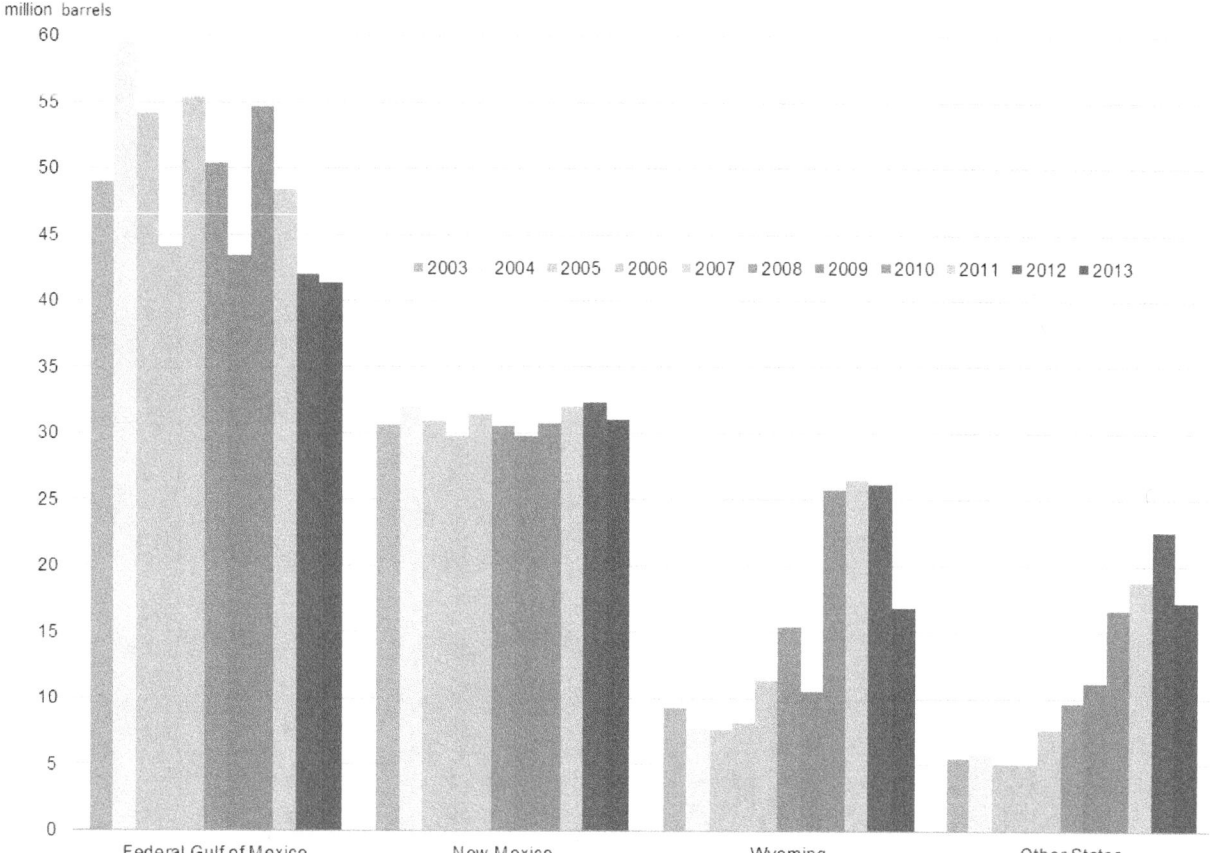

Source: U.S. Energy Information Administration based on U.S. Department of the Interior, Office of Natural Resources Revenue. "ONNR Statistical Information Site" (http://statistics.onrr.gov).

Figure 8. Coal production on federal and Indian lands, FY 2003-13

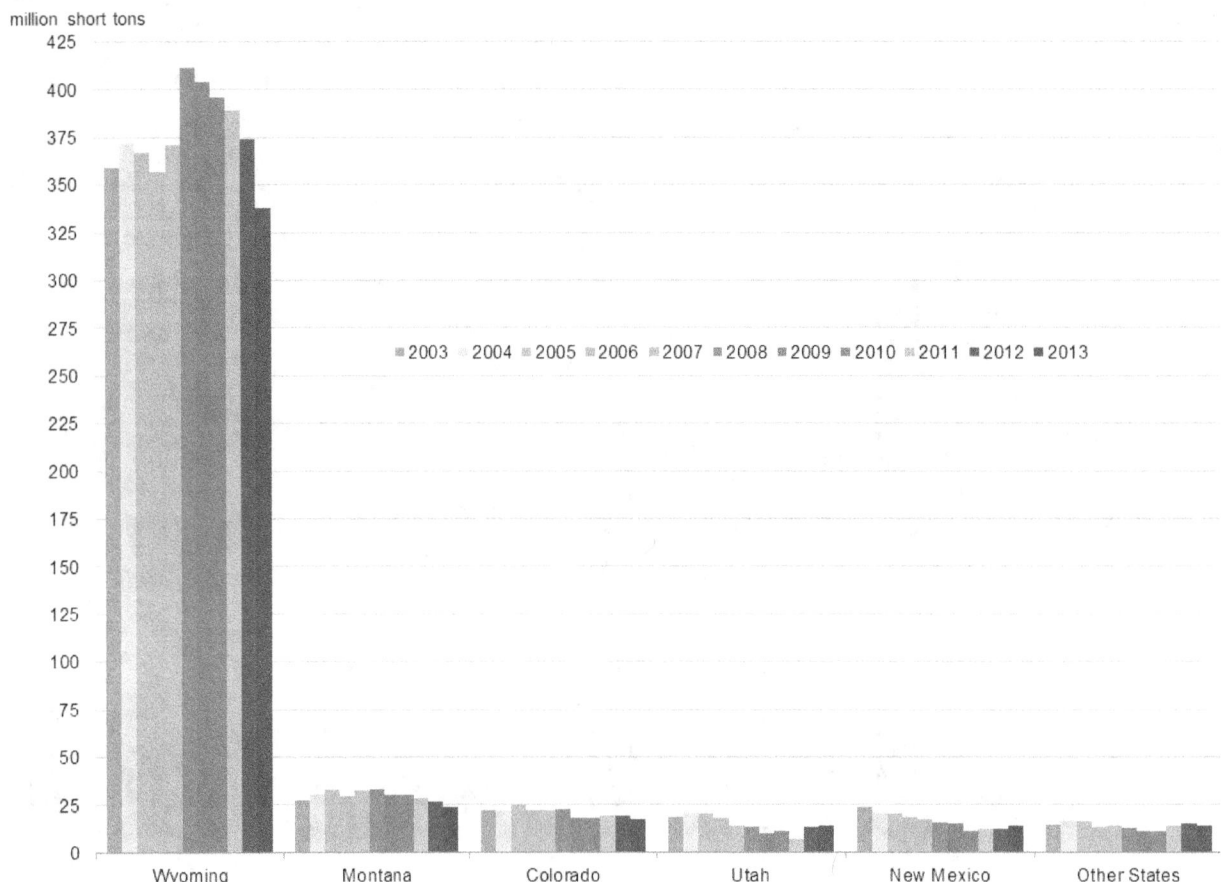

Source: U.S. Energy Information Administration based on U.S. Department of the Interior, Office of Natural Resources Revenue. "ONNR Statistical Information Site" (http://statistics.onrr.gov).

Table 3. Sales of crude oil and lease condensate production from federal and Indian lands, FY 2003-13

million barrels

Fiscal Year	Offshore Federal	Onshore Federal	Total Federal	Indian Lands
2003	579	100	679	10
2004	573	97	670	10
2005	542	96	638	10
2006	471	100	571	10
2007	514	104	618	10
2008	462	103	565	10
2009	543	104	647	10
2010	614	108	722	13
2011	518	113	631	20
2012	477	124	601	31
2013	473	133	606	46

Notes: Totals may not equal sum of components because of independent rounding. Onshore federal excludes volumes on Indian lands. Offshore federal only includes areas in federal waters.
Source: U.S. Energy Information Administration based on U.S. Department of the Interior, Office of Natural Resources Revenue. "ONNR Statistical Information Site" (http://statistics.onrr.gov).

Table 4. Sales of natural gas production from federal and Indian lands, FY 2003-13

billion cubic feet

Fiscal Year	Offshore Federal	Onshore Federal	Total Federal	Indian Lands
2003	4,523	2,276	6,799	283
2004	4,025	2,351	6,376	312
2005	3,522	2,535	6,057	326
2006	2,754	2,618	5,372	308
2007	2,701	2,857	5,558	284
2008	2,486	3,049	5,535	272
2009	2,213	3,168	5,381	266
2010	2,066	3,021	5,087	251
2011	1,678	2,919	4,597	254
2012	1,360	2,923	4,283	252
2013	1,180	2,663	3,843	239

Notes: Totals may not equal sum of components because of independent rounding. Onshore federal excludes volumes on Indian lands. Offshore federal only includes areas in federal waters.
Source: U.S. Energy Information Administration based on U.S. Department of the Interior, Office of Natural Resources Revenue. "ONNR Statistical Information Site" (http://statistics.onrr.gov).

Table 5. Sales of natural gas plant liquids production from federal and Indian lands, FY 2003-13

million barrels

Fiscal Year	Offshore Federal	Onshore Federal	Total Federal	Indian Lands
2003	51	42	93	2
2004	62	41	103	2
2005	56	40	96	2
2006	46	39	85	2
2007	59	44	103	3
2008	53	50	103	3
2009	45	47	92	3
2010	58	67	125	3
2011	50	72	122	3
2012	44	75	119	4
2013	44	59	103	4

Notes: Totals may not equal sum of components because of independent rounding. Onshore federal excludes volumes on Indian lands. Offshore federal only includes areas in federal waters.

Source: U.S. Energy Information Administration based on U.S. Department of the Interior, Office of Natural Resources Revenue. "ONNR Statistical Information Site" (http://statistics.onrr.gov).

Table 6. Sales of fossil fuel production from federal and Indian lands by state/area, FY 2003-13

trillion Btu

State	2003	2004	2005	2006	2007	2008	2009	2010	2011	2012	2013
Alabama	75	57	51	47	40	42	60	88	86	71	45
Alaska	61	66	68	52	32	28	27	27	25	22	20
Arizona	258	273	280	193	180	163	157	154	164	163	167
Arkansas	7	8	10	10	10	11	15	18	14	12	11
California	141	125	125	139	146	129	116	115	122	125	120
Colorado	785	842	960	906	904	932	846	855	916	949	872
Florida	0	-	-	-	-	-	-	-	-	-	-
Illinois	0	0	0	0	0	0	0	0	0	0	0
Indiana	0	0	0	0	-	-	0	0	0	0	0
Kansas	12	11	11	12	10	10	10	9	9	7	6
Kentucky	0	0	0	6	18	8	4	1	3	5	6
Louisiana	225	245	188	164	167	162	146	127	117	110	105
Michigan	4	4	4	4	4	4	3	3	2	2	2
Mississippi	19	19	18	16	16	17	14	13	13	12	12
Montana	612	684	722	661	723	727	662	659	612	576	514
Nebraska	0	0	1	2	1	0	0	0	0	0	0
Nevada	3	3	3	2	2	2	3	3	2	2	2
New Mexico	1,823	1,748	1,695	1,626	1,570	1,472	1,444	1,328	1,338	1,377	1,403
New York	0	0	0	0	0	0	0	0	0	0	0
North Dakota	70	92	88	111	121	126	77	83	164	288	371
Offshore Gulf	7,570	7,084	6,483	5,289	5,553	5,049	5,225	5,557	4,607	4,059	3,858
Offshore Pacific	170	156	145	144	138	131	129	123	108	92	98
Ohio	1	1	1	1	1	1	1	1	1	1	0
Oklahoma	56	57	55	57	59	57	60	60	63	60	57
Pennsylvania	0	0	0	0	0	0	0	0	0	0	0
South Dakota	1	1	1	1	1	1	1	1	1	1	1
Texas	119	113	90	87	87	67	64	49	54	74	58
Utah	586	637	676	654	621	647	622	632	572	733	731
Virginia	0	0	1	1	0	0	0	0	0	0	0
Washington	4	0	-	0	-	-	-	-	-	-	-
West Virginia	1	1	1	2	1	1	1	1	1	0	0
Wyoming	8,596	8,863	8,813	8,653	9,197	10,198	10,048	9,905	9,661	9,325	8,393
Total	**21,200**	**21,092**	**20,490**	**18,840**	**19,606**	**19,986**	**19,735**	**19,812**	**18,654**	**18,066**	**16,854**

Note: Totals may not equal sum of components because of independent rounding.

Source: U.S. Energy Information Administration based on U.S. Department of the Interior, Office of Natural Resources Revenue. "ONNR Statistical Information Site" (http://statistics.onrr.gov)

Table 7. Sales of crude oil and lease condensate production from federal and Indian lands by state/area, FY 2003-13

million barrels

State	2003	2004	2005	2006	2007	2008	2009	2010	2011	2012	2013
Alabama	0	0	0	0	0	0	0	0	0	0	0
Alaska	4	5	5	3	0	0	0	1	1	1	1
Arizona	0	0	0	0	0	0	0	0	0	0	0
Arkansas	0	-	-	-	-	-	-	-	-	-	-
California	23	21	21	23	24	21	19	19	19	19	19
Colorado	4	4	5	6	5	5	5	4	4	5	4
Florida	0	-	-	-	-	-	-	-	-	-	-
Illinois	0	0	0	0	0	0	0	0	0	0	0
Indiana	0	0	0	0	-	-	0	0	0	0	0
Kansas	0	0	0	1	0	0	0	0	0	0	0
Kentucky	0	0	0	0	0	0	0	0	0	0	0
Louisiana	13	13	8	7	7	7	7	7	6	7	7
Michigan	0	0	0	0	0	0	0	0	0	0	0
Mississippi	1	0	0	0	0	0	0	0	0	0	0
Montana	4	4	4	4	4	4	4	4	3	3	3
Nebraska	0	0	0	0	0	0	0	0	0	0	0
Nevada	0	0	0	0	0	0	0	0	0	0	0
New Mexico	32	30	26	25	25	26	28	31	35	42	51
New York	-	-	-	-	-	-	-	-	-	-	-
North Dakota	6	6	6	7	7	7	8	12	19	33	46
Offshore Gulf	531	527	502	435	480	430	512	584	490	451	447
Offshore Pacific	23	22	20	20	19	19	19	18	16	14	15
Ohio	0	0	0	0	0	0	0	0	0	0	0
Oklahoma	1	1	1	1	1	1	1	1	1	2	1
Pennsylvania	0	0	-	-	-	-	0	0	0	0	0
South Dakota	0	0	0	0	0	0	0	0	0	0	0
Texas	1	1	1	1	1	1	1	1	1	1	0
Utah	10	10	12	13	14	16	17	18	19	19	21
Virginia	-	-	-	-	-	-	-	-	-	-	-
Washington	-	-	-	-	-	-	-	-	-	-	-
West Virginia	-	-	-	0	-	-	-	-	-	-	-
Wyoming	34	34	34	35	36	36	35	35	35	35	35
Total	**689**	**680**	**648**	**581**	**627**	**575**	**657**	**736**	**651**	**632**	**652**

Note: Totals may not equal sum of components because of independent rounding.
Source: U.S. Energy Information Administration based on U.S. Department of the Interior, Office of Natural Resources Revenue. "ONNR Statistical Information Site" (http://statistics.onrr.gov).

Table 8. Sales of natural gas production from federal and Indian lands by state/area, FY 2003-13

billion cubic feet

State	2003	2004	2005	2006	2007	2008	2009	2010	2011	2012	2013
Alabama	71	53	48	44	36	34	30	32	27	20	21
Alaska	35	37	40	35	28	25	24	20	16	16	13
Arizona	0	0	0	0	0	0	0	0	0	0	-
Arkansas	7	8	9	10	10	10	15	18	14	12	10
California	6	5	5	7	7	7	7	7	10	12	8
Colorado	290	348	406	404	412	425	432	424	460	485	468
Florida	-	-	-	-	-	-	-	-	-	-	-
Illinois	-	-	-	-	-	-	-	-	-	-	-
Indiana	-	-	-	-	-	-	-	-	-	-	-
Kansas	11	10	9	8	8	8	7	7	6	5	4
Kentucky	0	0	0	0	0	0	0	0	0	0	0
Louisiana	140	161	132	116	111	108	96	79	73	66	61
Michigan	4	4	4	4	4	3	3	2	2	2	1
Mississippi	15	16	15	13	14	15	12	11	11	10	9
Montana	22	26	30	34	34	33	31	27	23	18	14
Nebraska	0	-	1	2	1	0	0	-	0	0	0
Nevada	-	-	-	-	-	-	-	-	-	-	-
New Mexico	1,005	996	985	965	926	874	846	788	758	748	702
New York	0	0	0	0	0	0	0	0	0	0	0
North Dakota	8	8	9	10	10	9	8	9	10	14	20
Offshore Gulf	4,194	3,706	3,277	2,534	2,495	2,306	2,046	1,921	1,555	1,257	1,086
Offshore Pacific	32	27	25	26	25	21	20	20	15	12	12
Ohio	1	1	1	1	1	1	1	1	0	0	0
Oklahoma	32	32	32	34	33	33	39	39	40	39	34
Pennsylvania	0	0	0	0	0	0	0	0	0	0	0
South Dakota	0	0	0	0	0	0	0	0	0	0	0
Texas	108	102	80	76	75	58	57	43	47	67	53
Utah	135	147	188	209	243	270	300	281	292	316	290
Virginia	0	0	1	1	0	0	0	0	0	0	0
Washington	-	-	-	-	-	-	-	-	-	-	-
West Virginia	1	1	1	2	1	1	1	1	1	0	-
Wyoming	965	998	1,084	1,144	1,367	1,564	1,672	1,608	1,490	1,434	1,275
Total	7,082	6,688	6,384	5,680	5,842	5,806	5,647	5,338	4,851	4,535	4,082

Note: Totals may not equal sum of components because of independent rounding.

Source: U.S. Energy Information Administration based on U.S. Department of the Interior, Office of Natural Resources Revenue. "ONRR Statistical Information Site" (http://statistics.onrr.gov).

Table 9. Sales of natural gas plant liquids production from federal and Indian lands by state/area, FY 2003-13

million barrels

State	2003	2004	2005	2006	2007	2008	2009	2010	2011	2012	2013
Alabama	0	0	0	0	1	1	1	1	1	1	1
Alaska	0	0	0	0	0	0	0	-	0	0	-
Arizona	-	-	-	-	-	-	0	0	0	0	-
Arkansas	-	-	-	-	-	-	-	-	-	-	-
California	0	0	0	0	0	0	0	0	0	0	0
Colorado	1	1	1	1	1	3	5	7	9	11	6
Florida	-	-	-	-	-	-	-	-	-	-	-
Illinois	-	-	-	-	-	-	-	-	-	-	-
Indiana	-	-	-	-	-	-	-	-	-	-	-
Kansas	0	0	0	0	0	0	0	0	0	0	0
Kentucky	-	-	-	-	-	-	0	0	0	-	-
Louisiana	1	2	2	1	3	3	1	2	1	1	1
Michigan	0	0	0	0	0	0	0	0	0	0	0
Mississippi	-	-	-	-	-	-	-	-	-	0	0
Montana	0	0	0	0	0	0	0	0	0	0	0
Nebraska	-	-	-	-	-	0	-	-	-	-	-
Nevada	-	-	-	-	-	-	-	-	-	-	-
New Mexico	31	32	31	30	31	31	30	31	32	32	31
New York	-	-	-	-	-	-	-	-	-	-	-
North Dakota	0	0	0	0	0	0	0	0	1	1	1
Offshore Gulf	49	60	54	44	55	50	43	55	48	42	41
Offshore Pacific	0	0	0	0	0	0	0	0	0	0	0
Ohio	-	-	-	-	-	-	-	-	-	-	-
Oklahoma	0	0	0	0	0	0	0	0	0	1	0
Pennsylvania	-	-	-	-	-	-	-	-	-	-	0
South Dakota	-	-	-	-	-	-	-	-	-	-	-
Texas	0	0	0	0	0	0	0	0	0	0	0
Utah	1	1	1	1	1	2	3	5	6	7	7
Virginia	-	-	-	-	-	-	-	-	-	-	-
Washington	-	-	-	-	-	-	-	-	-	-	-
West Virginia	-	-	-	-	-	-	-	-	-	-	-
Wyoming	9	8	8	8	11	15	11	26	27	26	17
Total	**94**	**105**	**98**	**87**	**106**	**106**	**95**	**128**	**126**	**123**	**106**

Note: Totals may not equal sum of components because of independent rounding.
Source: U.S. Energy Information Administration based on U.S. Department of the Interior, Office of Natural Resources Revenue. "ONNR Statistical Information Site" (http://statistics.onrr.gov).

Table 10. Sales of coal production from federal and Indian lands, FY 2003-13

million short tons

State	2003	2004	2005	2006	2007	2008	2009	2010	2011	2012	2013
Alabama	-	0	-	0	0	0	1	3	3	2	1
Alaska	-	-	-	-	-	-	-	-	-	-	-
Arizona	13	13	14	9	9	8	8	8	8	8	8
Arkansas	-	-	-	-	-	-	-	-	-	-	-
California	-	-	-	-	-	-	-	-	-	-	-
Colorado	22	22	25	22	22	23	18	18	19	19	17
Florida	-	-	-	-	-	-	-	-	-	-	-
Illinois	-	-	-	-	-	-	-	-	-	-	-
Indiana	-	-	-	-	-	-	-	-	-	-	-
Kansas	-	-	-	-	-	-	-	-	-	-	-
Kentucky	-	-	-	0	1	0	0	0	0	0	0
Louisiana	-	-	-	-	-	-	-	-	-	-	-
Michigan	-	-	-	-	-	-	-	-	-	-	-
Mississippi	-	-	-	-	-	-	-	-	-	-	-
Montana	28	31	33	30	33	33	30	30	28	27	24
Nebraska	-	-	-	-	-	-	-	-	-	-	-
Nevada	-	-	-	-	-	-	-	-	-	-	-
New Mexico	24	21	20	19	17	15	15	11	12	12	14
New York	-	-	-	-	-	-	-	-	-	-	-
North Dakota	1	2	2	3	3	4	1	0	2	4	4
Offshore Gulf	-	-	-	-	-	-	-	-	-	-	-
Offshore Pacific	-	-	-	-	-	-	-	-	-	-	-
Ohio	-	-	-	-	-	-	0	-	-	-	-
Oklahoma	1	1	1	1	1	1	1	1	1	0	1
Pennsylvania	-	-	-	-	-	-	-	-	-	-	-
South Dakota	-	-	-	-	-	-	-	-	-	-	-
Texas	-	-	-	-	-	-	-	-	-	-	-
Utah	19	21	20	18	14	14	10	11	7	13	14
Virginia	-	-	-	-	-	-	-	-	-	-	-
Washington	0	0	-	0	-	-	-	-	-	-	-
West Virginia	-	-	-	-	-	-	-	-	-	-	-
Wyoming	359	372	367	356	371	411	404	396	389	374	337
Total	**466**	**484**	**482**	**458**	**471**	**509**	**488**	**478**	**470**	**461**	**420**

Note: Totals may not equal sum of components because of independent rounding.
Source: U.S. Energy Information Administration based on U.S. Department of the Interior, Office of Natural Resources Revenue. "ONNR Statistical Information Site" (http://statistics.onrr.gov).

Appendix

State/area maps

Figure A1. Fossil fuel production on federal and Indian lands, FY 2013

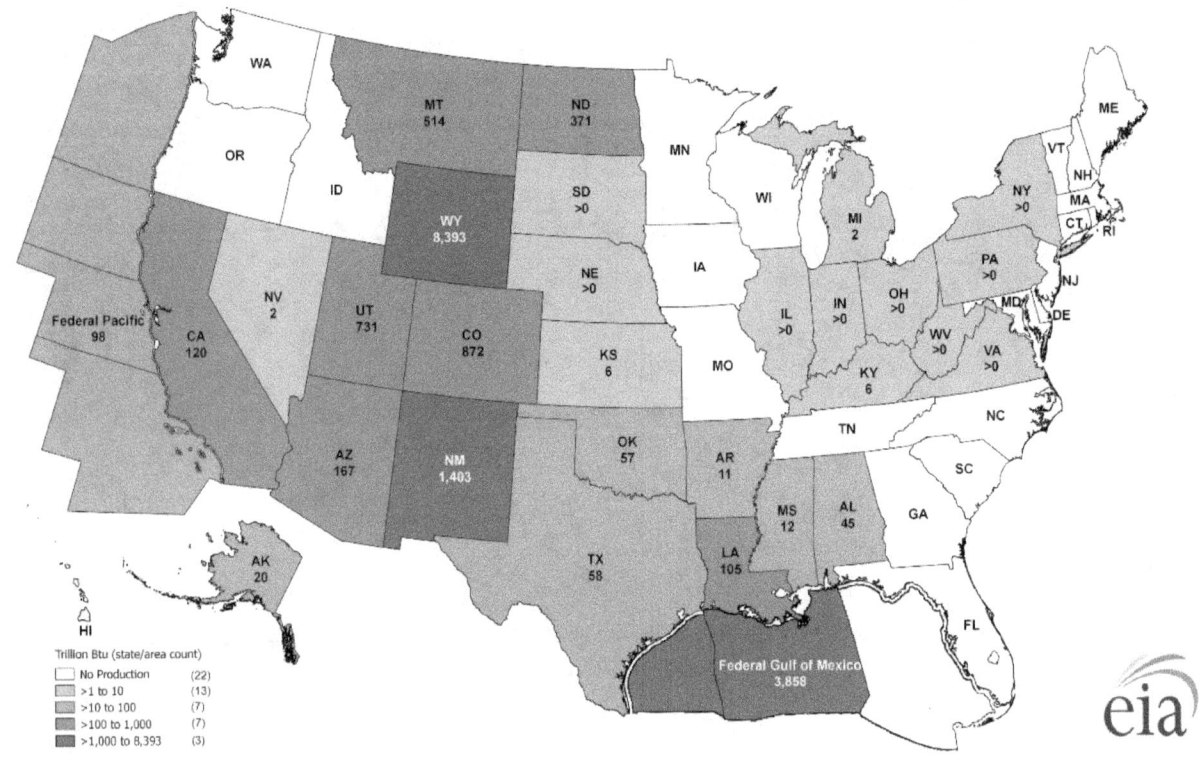

Source: U.S. Energy Information Administration based on U.S. Department of the Interior, Office of Natural Resources Revenue. "ONNR Statistical Information Site" (http://statistics.onrr.gov).

U.S. Energy Information Administration | Sales of Fossil Fuels Produced on Federal and Indian Lands, FY 2003 through FY 2013

23

Figure A2. Changes in fossil fuels production (trillion Btu) on federal and Indian lands, FY 2003-13

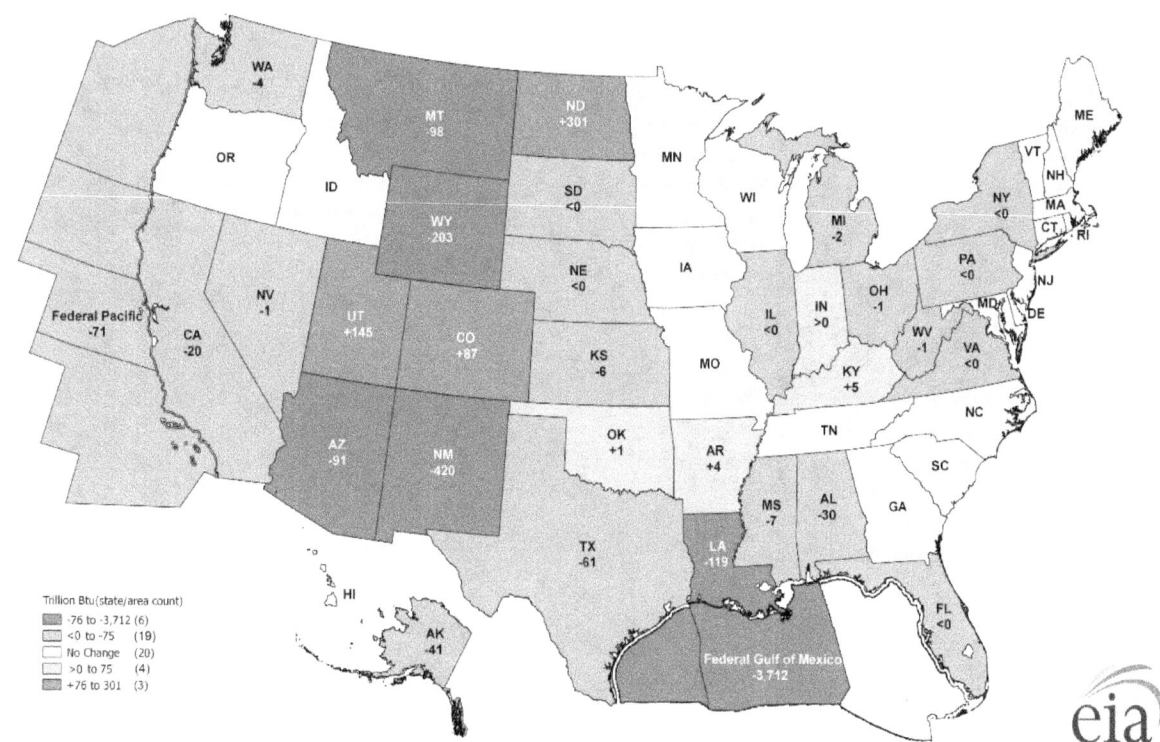

Source: U.S. Energy Information Administration based on U.S. Department of the Interior, Office of Natural Resources Revenue. "ONNR Statistical Information Site" (http://statistics.onrr.gov).

Figure A3. Crude oil production on federal and Indian lands, FY 2013

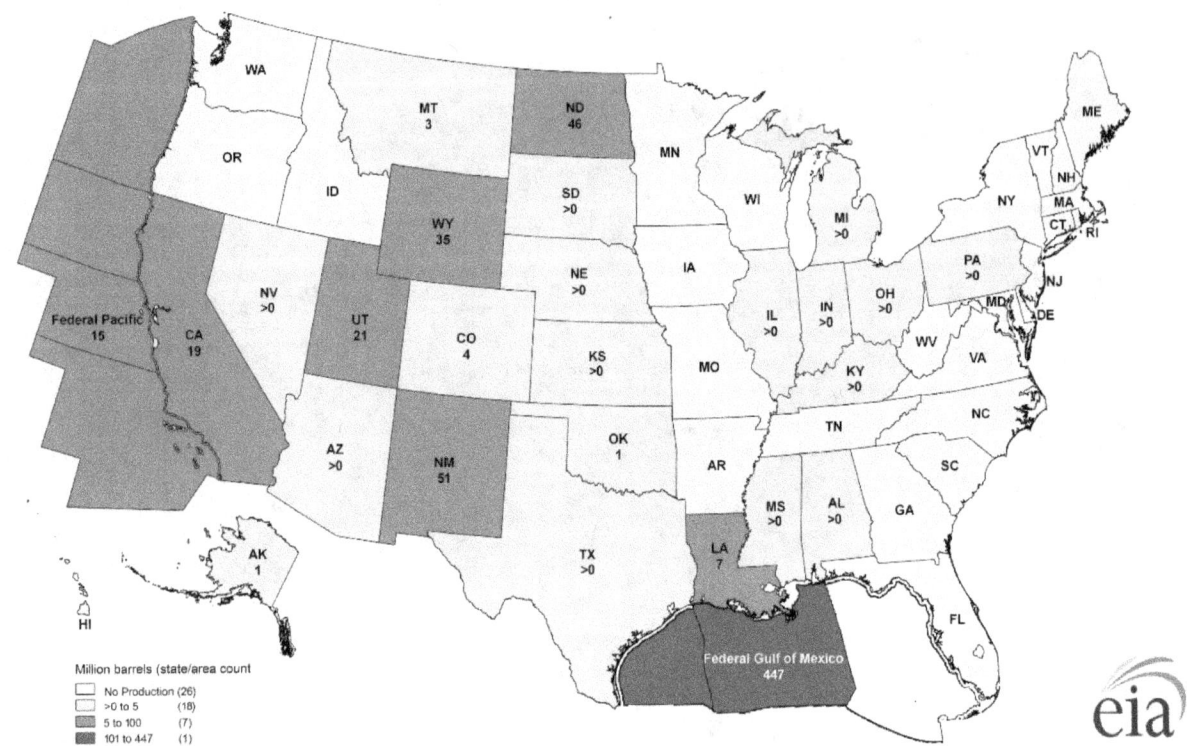

Source: U.S. Energy Information Administration based on U.S. Department of the Interior, Office of Natural Resources Revenue. "ONNR Statistical Information Site" (http://statistics.onrr.gov).

Figure A4. Changes in crude oil production on federal and Indian lands, FY 2003-13

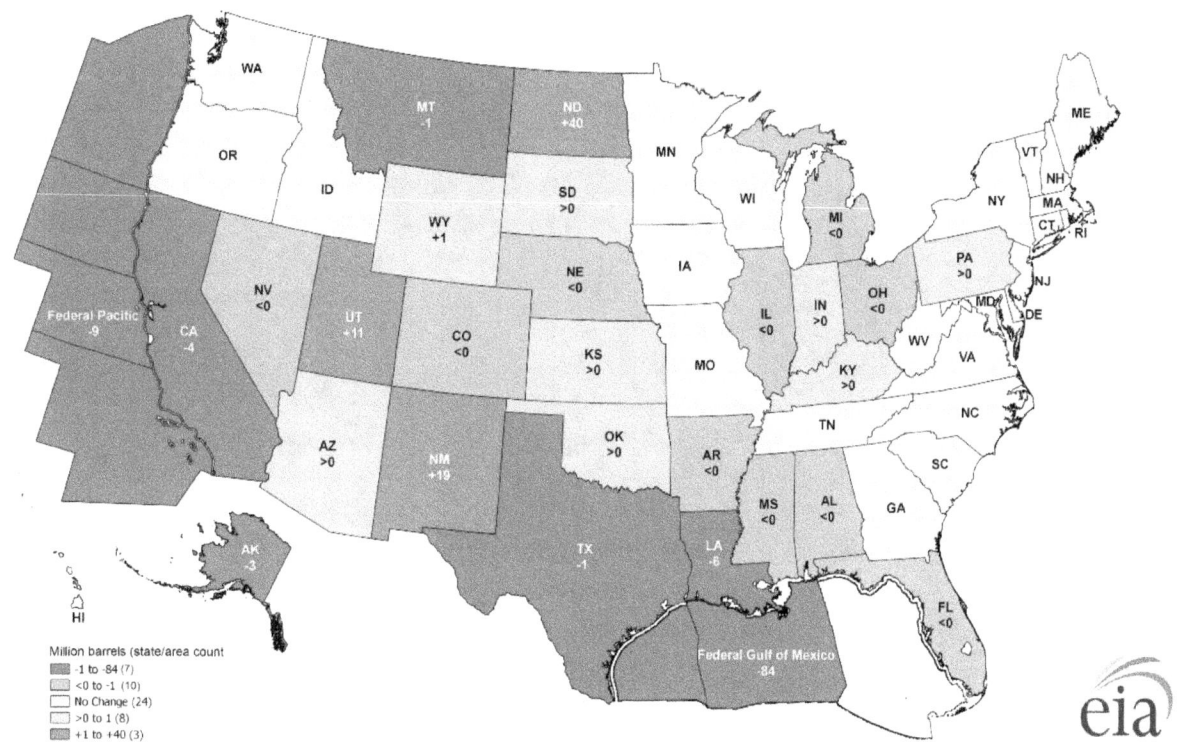

Million barrels (state/area count)
- -1 to -84 (7)
- <0 to -1 (10)
- No Change (24)
- >0 to 1 (8)
- +1 to +40 (3)

Source: U.S. Energy Information Administration based on U.S. Department of the Interior, Office of Natural Resources Revenue. "ONNR Statistical Information Site" (http://statistics.onrr.gov).

Figure A5. Natural gas production on federal and Indian lands, FY 2013

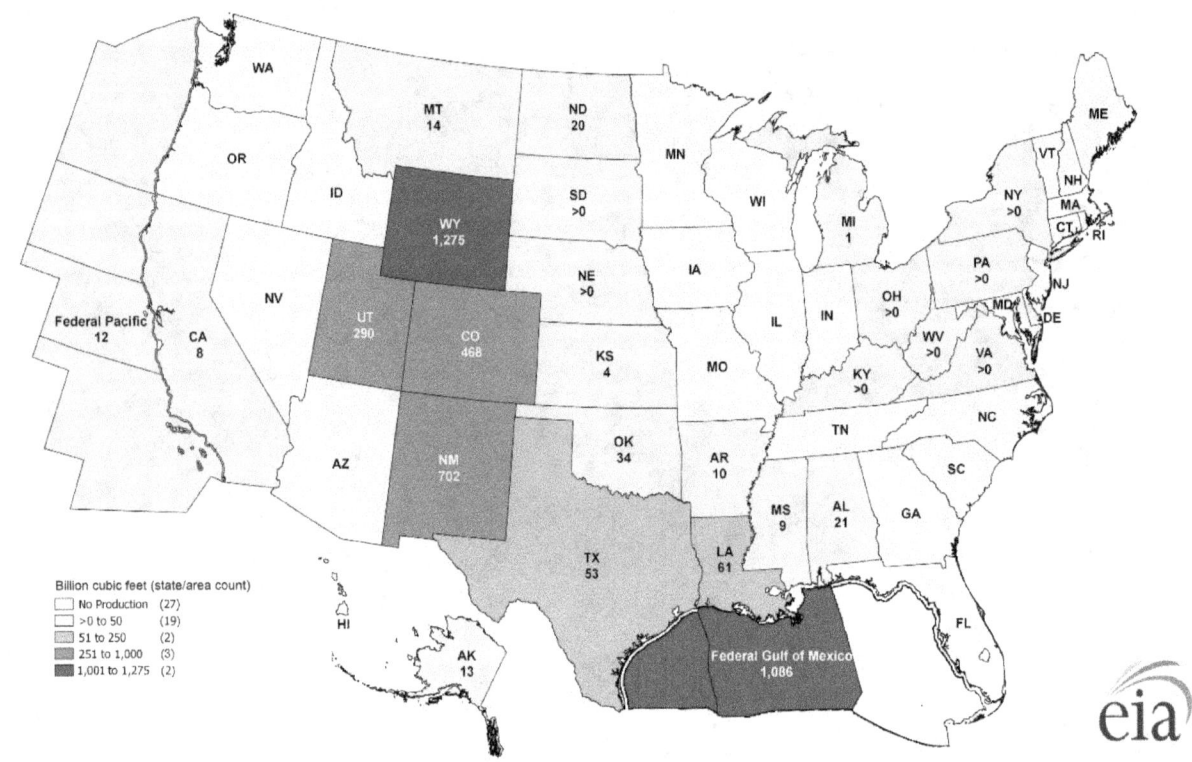

Source: U.S. Energy Information Administration based on U.S. Department of the Interior, Office of Natural Resources Revenue. "ONNR Statistical Information Site" (http://statistics.onrr.gov).

Figure A6. Changes in natural gas production on federal and Indian lands, FY 2003-13

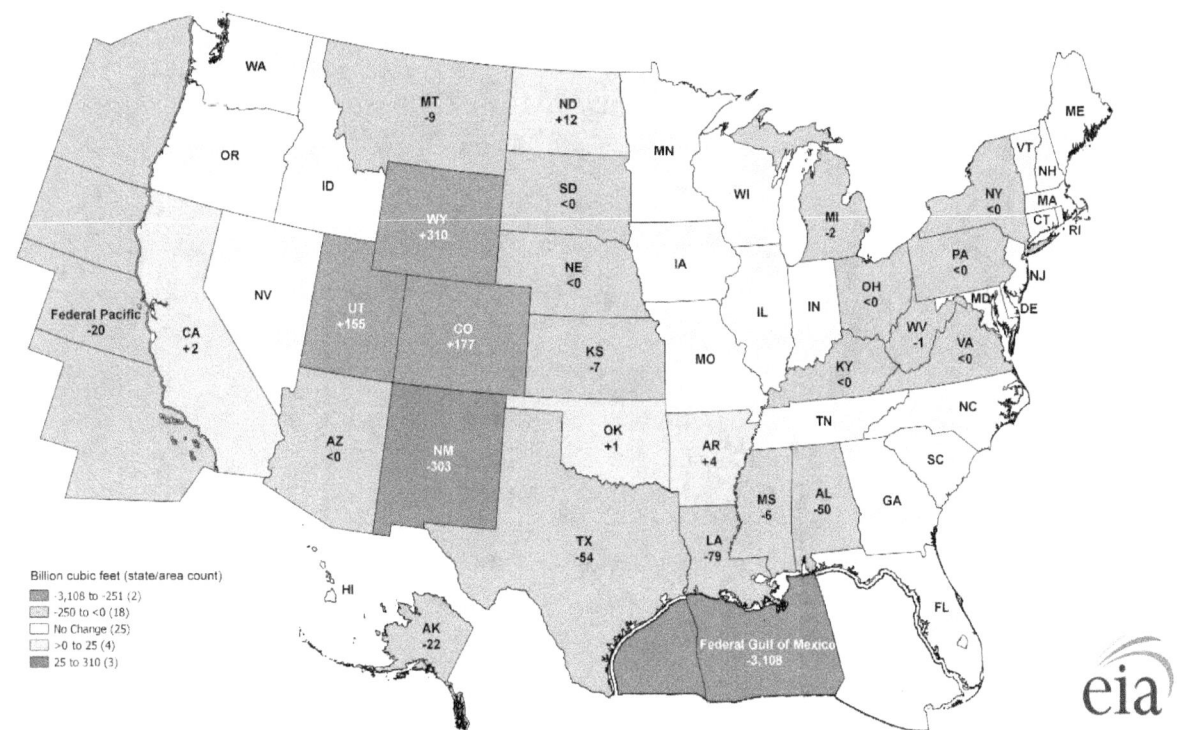

Source: U.S. Energy Information Administration based on U.S. Department of the Interior, Office of Natural Resources Revenue. "ONNR Statistical Information Site" (http://statistics.onrr.gov).

Figure A7. Natural gas liquids production on federal and Indian lands, FY 2013

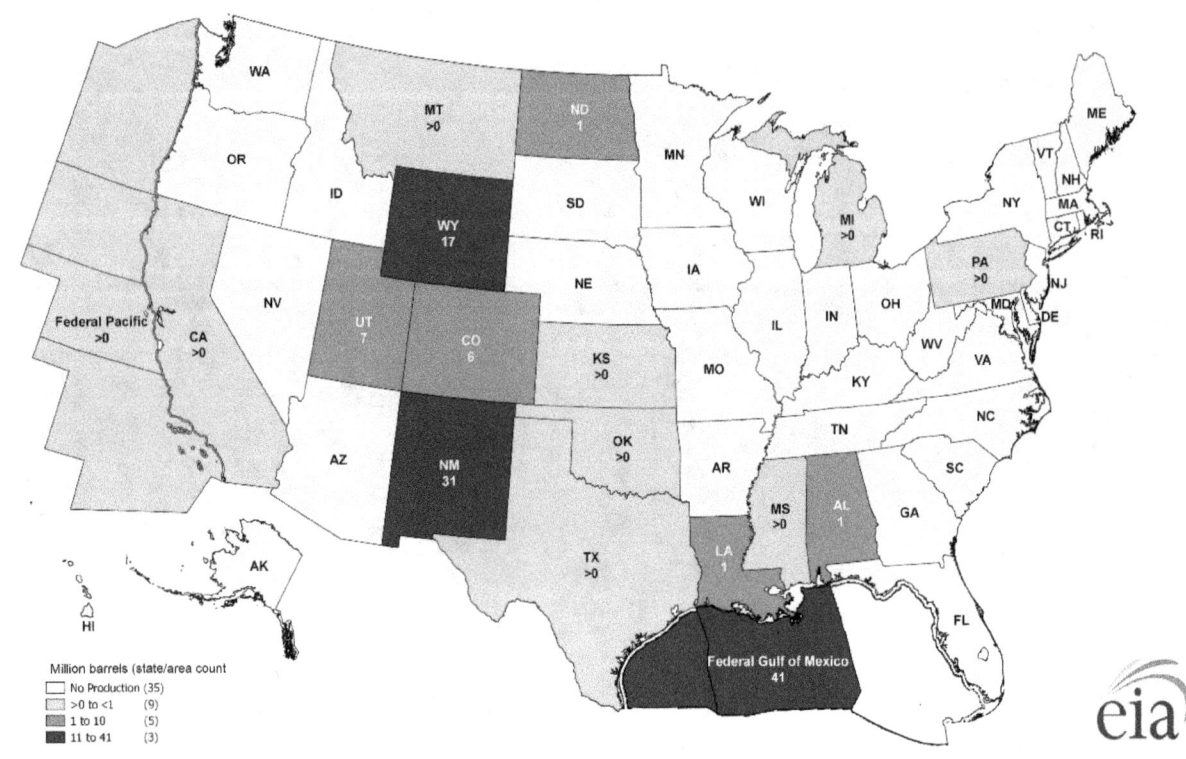

Million barrels (state/area count)

☐ No Production	(35)
☐ >0 to <1	(9)
☐ 1 to 10	(5)
■ 11 to 41	(3)

Source: U.S. Energy Information Administration based on U.S. Department of the Interior, Office of Natural Resources Revenue. "ONNR Statistical Information Site" (http://statistics.onrr.gov).

Figure A8. Changes in natural gas liquids production on federal and Indian lands, FY 2003-13

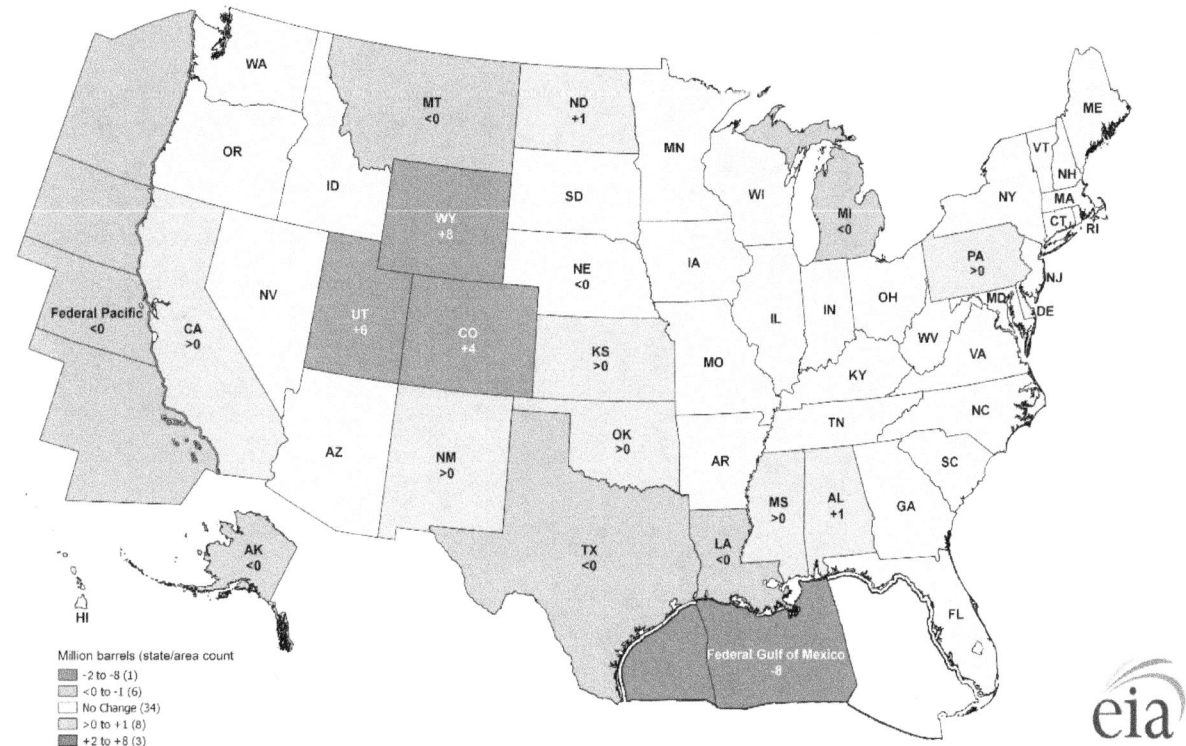

Source: U.S. Energy Information Administration based on U.S. Department of the Interior, Office of Natural Resources Revenue. "ONNR Statistical Information Site" (http://statistics.onrr.gov).

Figure A9. Coal production on federal and Indian lands, FY 2013

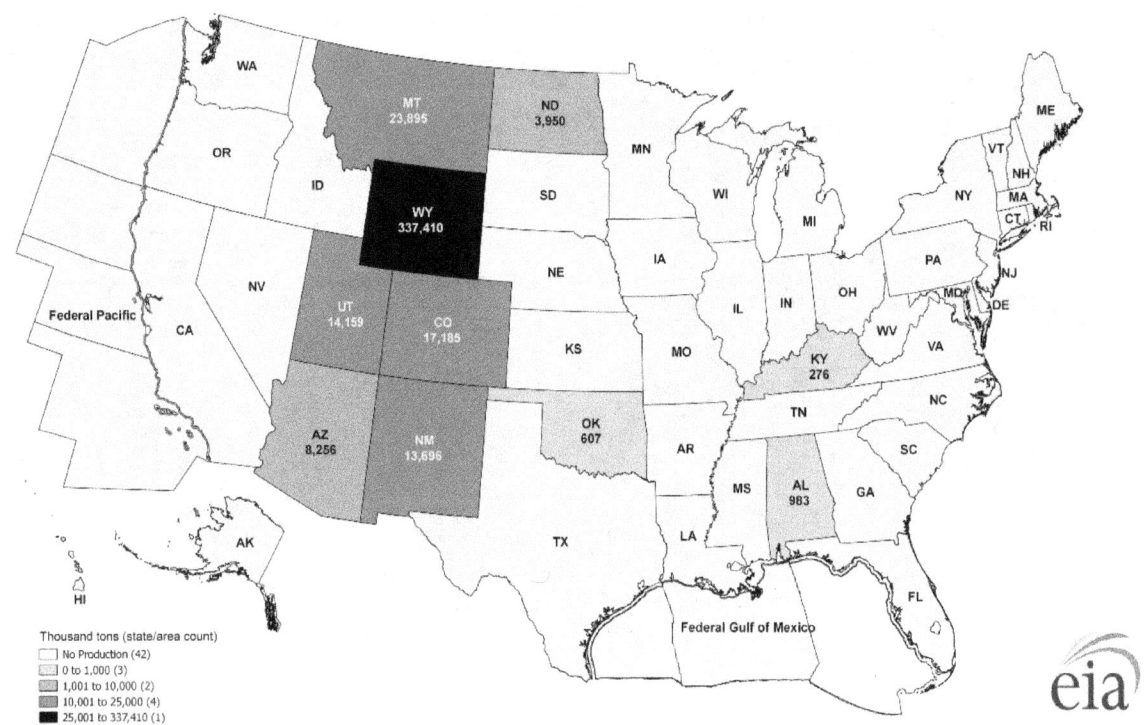

Thousand tons (state/area count)
- No Production (42)
- 0 to 1,000 (3)
- 1,001 to 10,000 (2)
- 10,001 to 25,000 (4)
- 25,001 to 337,410 (1)

Source: U.S. Energy Information Administration based on U.S. Department of the Interior, Office of Natural Resources Revenue. "ONNR Statistical Information Site" (http://statistics.onrr.gov).

Figure A10. Changes in coal production on federal and Indian lands by state, FY 2003-13

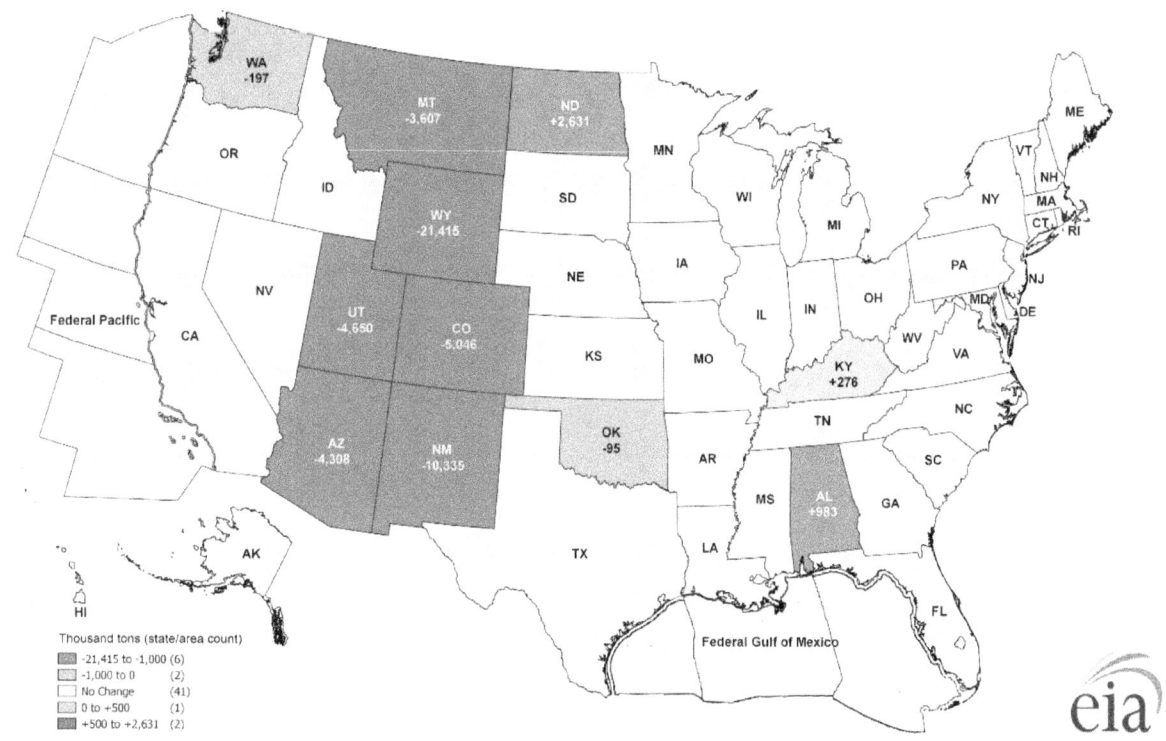

Thousand tons (state/area count)

▨	-21,415 to -1,000	(6)
▨	-1,000 to 0	(2)
☐	No Change	(41)
▨	0 to +500	(1)
■	+500 to +2,631	(2)

Source: U.S. Energy Information Administration based on U.S. Department of the Interior, Office of Natural Resources Revenue. "ONNR Statistical Information Site" (http://statistics.onrr.gov).